The Family Dinner

The Family Dinner

A Celebration of Love, Laughter, and Leftovers

Linda Sunshine
and Mary Tiegreen

Clarkson Potter/Publishers
New York

Published by Clarkson Potter/Publishers, New York, New York.
Member of the Crown Publishing Group, a division of Random House, Inc.
www.randomhouse.com

Permissions and photo credits appear on page 111.

CLARKSON N. POTTER is a trademark and POTTER and colophon are registered trademarks of Random House, Inc.

Printed in Singapore

Design by Mary Tiegreen

Library of Congress Cataloging-in-Publication Data
Sunshine, Linda.
    The family dinner : a celebration of love, laughter, and leftovers /
Linda Sunshine and Mary Tiegreen.
    1. Family—United States—Case studies.   2. Dinners and dining.
I. Tiegreen, Mary.   II. Title.
    HQ536.S875   2003
    306.85'0973—dc21   2002004322

ISBN 1-4000-4592-4

10   9   8   7   6   5   4   3   2   1

First Edition

Janet

Norma

Jacqueline

To Norma Deutsch Sunshine,
Janet O'Meara and Jacqueline Pedroli
for cooking our family dinners with laughter
and loving grace . . .

POKER FACE

This is a book about how family dinners establish the rhythm of family life and define who we are, where we came from, and where we might expect to be going. The common thread in these stories is how we come to understand the rituals of our childhood at the dinner table.

Each of the stories in this book is profound and unique. Each of them represents a particular family at a particular moment in time. There are as many different stories, I suppose, as there are families. Here is mine.

Our family dinners always took place at my Aunt Hannah's house in Woodmere, Long Island. Our drive from Fair Lawn, New Jersey, was long and tedious, so we arrived there tired and cranky, my mother always complaining about how it would be nice for a change if, just once, the family came out to New Jersey. She eventually got her wish, but only after Aunt Hannah died.

We were a noisy, hungry bunch of people. By the time dinner was served, the house was jammed with aunts, uncles, and cousins; the dining-room table was extended to full length and, in the adjoining living room, folding card tables were set up for the kids.

Dinner was an endless succession of rich foods and even richer stories, which, like mantras, were endlessly repeated. Each adult had a legend all his or her own. As a young woman, my mother once bought a dress for $9.96 when she had only $10 in her purse and had to beg for a penny from a nice policeman to pay for her nickel subway ride home. Caught in a great blizzard, my father once had to walk six miles through three feet of snow to get home from work. When he came through the door, my mother's first words to him were about how she was worried about her brother Eddie. It occurs to me now, decades later, that so many of our family stories were about the struggles to get home.

There were stories of the grandparents we never knew and our infamous Uncle Abe, the senator from Albany, who'd been involved in some mysterious scandal that no one ever fully explained to the children. Brooklyn life during the Great Depression became as real to me as my own childhood. Back then, I did not realize that these stories were precious gifts. At the kids' tables, we rolled our eyes heavenward, dumbstruck by how the adults were trapped in some weird time warp, always discussing the past.

It didn't really matter. We were all just biding our time until the meal ended. The highlight of our family dinners, always, came after the food.

Finally, the dining-room table was cleared down to its padded plastic covering. Cakes, cookies, candies, and the pot of coffee were removed to the sideboard. Wallets and cigarettes were fetched from our parents' purses and coat pockets. Ashtrays were strewn around the table, along with unopened decks of cards and poker chips. My father took charge of the "bank" and exchanged chips for money. Everyone stacked their chips and quarters in neat piles between their elbows. The talking never stopped, so eventually either Uncle Bernie or Uncle Sol would pound on the table impatiently and say, "Come on already! Deal the cards!"

It was time for the poker game to begin.

My family did not do sports. We didn't play board games. We did not picnic. We did not play tennis or golf. We did not ride bikes. We didn't throw footballs or baseballs. In fact, we didn't go outdoors much. We stayed inside, ate large meals, told stories, smoked cigarettes, and played cards.

The adults in my family loved poker and their legacy to us was the laughter and excitement of the game. Poker was serious business, a game of skill when the cards came your way and of serious bluffing when they didn't. After each hand, there was a lot of discussion and analysis of strategy. And because money was involved, there were important lessons to be learned. The children—there were nine cousins in all—were allowed to play, but only if we "acted like adults." There would be no crying over lost hands, no temper tantrums for mistakes or rotten luck. (Though the adults had no such No Tantrum rule for themselves.) Go for the inside straight and you got reprimanded for the sucker play and throughout the night were scolded for bad judgment. Once I was dealt four kings in five-card draw and jumped out of my chair with joy. Big mistake. Everyone at the table folded, leaving behind a pitiful pot. I learned to curb my enthusiasm.

If you lost all your money, you were out of the game, but, on this issue, my ace in the hole was my mother. She was an easy touch, and over loud protests, she'd toss me handfuls of change when my stash was gone. "She'll never learn how to handle money if you keep doing that," my father would tell her, but my mother would wave him off with a flick of her hand.

The poker game lasted well into the early hours of the morning. Too tired to drive home, we spent the night in Woodmere, sprawled out on couches and doubled or tripled up in the beds. We returned to New Jersey late in the afternoon of the next day, our pants unbuttoned to accommodate our expanded stomachs. Long before the car crossed over the George Washington Bridge, I fell asleep in the backseat, more often than not my pockets bulging with quarters. I never drew to an inside straight, and by the age of ten I'd perfected the poker face. I once bluffed my cousin Joel's full house with two pair, creating a family legend of my own, but as my father predicted, I never did learn how to handle my money.

Linda Sunshine
February 2002

Call it a clan, call it a network, call it a tribe, call it a family. Whatever you call it, whoever you are, you need one.

Jane Howard
Families (1978)

The common thread

T he family. We are a strange little band of characters trudging through life sharing diseases and toothpaste, coveting one another's desserts, hiding shampoo, borrowing money, locking each other out of our rooms, inflicting pain and kissing to heal it in the same instant, loving, laughing, defending, and trying to figure out the common thread that bound us all together.

Erma Bombeck
Family—The Ties That Bind . . . and Gag! (1987)

The noisiest table in heaven

For me there will be no heaven unless it is laid out around a round oak table turned oblong by company's-coming leaves and stretched into infinity to accommodate those who have gathered joyfully, eagerly, around Kentucky tables here on earth.

At this table I will, of course, find the relatives and family friends who nourished and nurtured me as a child. My Aunt Ariel will be presiding over the world's finest jam cake while Aunt Johnny slips me a handful of red and yellow "tommytoes," still warm from the garden whose earth I can smell on her chapped but tender fingers. Charlie, my favorite uncle, will be crouched to the side, laughing and goading Daddy on to crank, crank, crank that freezer of homemade ice cream. And Ethel will be passing a big bowl of milky creamed corn, scraped from ears my Uncle Clifton has raised, and the perfect match for Jessie's white half-runner beans cooked long and slow to tender perfection.

There will be no rank strangers here—not for me or for anyone who cares to join us. As has been the custom through-out Kentucky's history, the table of my home state will always have room for anyone who is hungry and enough food to be divided up and shared until everyone there is fed.

How will you find us? Well, I'm afraid we will likely be the noisiest table in heaven.

Ronni Lundy
Foreword
Savory Memories (1998)

*The most remarkable thing about my
mother is that for thirty years she served
the family nothing but leftovers.
The original meal has
never been found.*

Calvin Trillin

What my mother believed about cooking is that if you worked hard and prospered, someone else would do it for you.

Nora Ephron

Poor Mother!

My name is Nicholas Fain Owen. I was born in Bristol, Tennessee, and currently live in Cherokee Park, Bluff City, Tennessee. When I was a child we lived in a big old eleven-room, two-story house. I was the runt of the litter in our family of twelve children, three of whom are younger than me. There were five boys and seven girls.... We always had two tables....

We had a big table with a bench on either side and a chair at the head and at the foot of the table. Dad sat at the head and Mother sat at the foot. We older children sat on each side of the benches. The younger ones, the first ones to eat at the first table, had to sit in the middle of the benches. So when we heard "Dinner's ready," or "Supper's ready," all the younger kids would start running so they could sit in the middle. If you didn't make it to the middle you had to wait for the next table.

The first ones would eat, the table was cleared and reset for the second table. This was done at every meal in our house. Poor Mother! She cooked breakfast and cleaned up and started dinner.

Nick and Marje Owen
Table Talk (1995)

Every night of my childhood

om cooked the steaks in her usual fashion, which was to put the meat in the broiler for about a minute, turn it, and announce that dinner was ready. . . .

Dad ate with his usual appetite. When he was done he turned to Mom and said, "What a wonderful dinner, darling. Thank you so much." And then he did what he had done every night of my childhood: kissed her hand.

Ruth Reichl
Tender at the Bone (1998)

Enough for her family to eat

The family meal was always served onto our plates by my father from serving platters, and when everyone had said grace and we all concluded "Amen," my mother would say, "Oh, John, you haven't left yourself anything but the carcass" (if it was a chicken), or "the head" (if it was a fish), or "the tail" (if it was a steak), or "the gristle" (if it was a roast). She was often right. My mother always felt that there wouldn't be enough for her family to eat. Food was so rich and so abundant in our house that even the pets were all overweight.

Susan Cheever
Home Before Dark (1984)

Sounds soothing

Inevitably, my mind kept turning to the time I first made a chicken, which sounds soothing but wasn't. I was seventeen. My mother talked me through it: season, truss, roast, let rest, carve. The only thing she left out was thaw. Even today, when family members have a little eggnog and want a good laugh, someone says, "Anna's chicken!" and they all roar and roll around while I have another drink.

Anna Quindlen
Living Out Loud (1988)

Most turkeys taste better the day after; my mother's tasted better the day before.

Rita Rudner

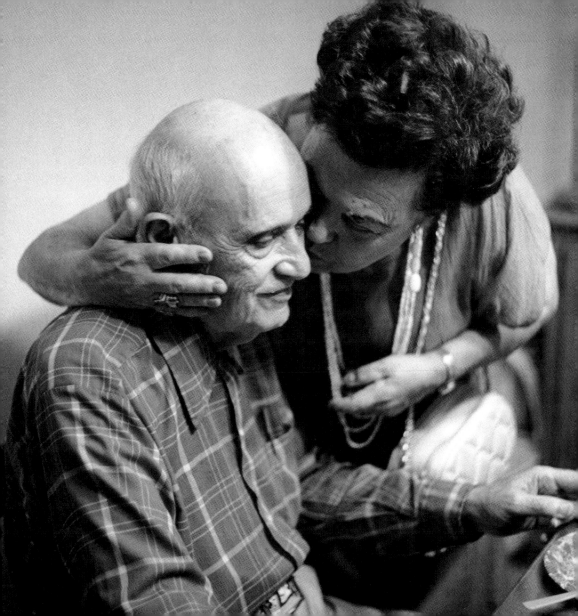

Memories of our family

We always find ways to celebrate our memories of our family and friends. Why, we still have a birthday party for Papa, even though he's been gone since 1928. We cook his favorite birthday meal, just the way he liked it: cheese and gravy, rice and sweet potatoes, ham, macaroni and cheese, cabbage, cauliflower, broccoli, turnips, and carrots. For dessert we'll have a birthday cake—a pound cake—and ambrosia, with oranges and fresh coconuts.

Sarah L. and A. Elizabeth Delany
Having Our Say (1993)

My father was the first man in his family to sit at a desk from Monday to Friday and use his head to support his wife and child.

On Sundays he sat at the head of the table and carved roast beef.

Glenda Adam
The Hottest Night of the Century (1989)

What Sundays smell like

At every Sunday dinner, in the middle of the table, in a bowl of water, floated a single magnolia blossom, cut from the tree in our front yard. Its perfume, layered between the chicken and the kale, is still what Sundays smell like. I have only to pass a magnolia tree in bloom and am transported back to #11 Innis Court, with its wide front porch, and the glider looking across the street to the broad flat lawn of the old folks' home, the Altenheim, and long afternoons idled away in delectable anticipation of the dinner hour.

Frederick Smock
"One Writer's Beginning"
Savory Memories (1998)

*You think you have a handle on God,
the Universe, and the Great White
Light until you go home for
Thanksgiving. In an hour,
you realize how far you've
got to go and who is
the real turkey.*

Shirley MacLaine
Dance While You Can (1991)

Pie, Fred?

My grandmother, when she served dinner, was a virtuoso hanging on the edge of her own ecstatic performance. . . . She was a little power crazed: she had us and, by God, we were going to eat. . . . The futility of saying no was supreme, and no one ever tried it. How could a son-in-law, already weakened near the point of imbecility by the once, twice, thrice charge of the barricades of pork and mashed potato, be expected to gather his feeble wit long enough to ignore the final call of his old commander when she sounded the alarm: "Pie, Fred?"

Patricia Hampl
A Romantic Education (1981)

When my mother had to get dinner for 8 she'd just make enough for 16 and only serve half.

Gracie Allen
News summaries
December 1, 1950

The resident Cute Kid

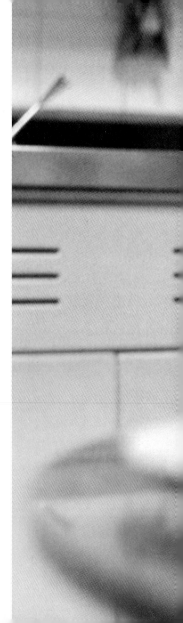

T o my chagrin, my status as resident Cute Kid had automatically anointed me the designated grace-sayer, so back when I was five or six years old, several of my aunts ganged up on me and made me memorize some perfunctory little rhyming pietism on the order of "Good bread, good meat! / Good God, let's eat!" which I dutifully rattled off before every Sunday dinner. With the  impending feast literally right under my nose, however, concentration was often hard to maintain, and I sometimes conferred my blessing so peremptorily that I forgot altogether what I was supposed to be saying. One Sunday, in place of my usual high-speed incantation, I heard myself solemnly intoning the Lord's Prayer; another time, the Pledge of Allegiance.

Ed McClanahan
"Grandma Jess's Easy East Rolls"
Savory Memories (1998)

"That went well"

T he door of the house opened and Doug's mother came out. She was plump and comfortable, with neatly set gray hair and sensible glasses. She wore an apron over a light blue print dress and she waved, as if we had traveled a great distance instead of the five miles that separated our apartment from their house.

We navigated the steps and stood there awkwardly. Doug and his mother did not kiss. "This is Ruth, Mom," said Doug, and she smiled. "Why, hello," she said, pointing into the house.

We went into the living room, which was almost filled by a pair of Barcaloungers, a large television set, and a coffee table. The corner of the coffee table ripped my stocking as I swerved around it; looking down I saw a *TV Guide* in a needlepoint cover. "My Aunt Winnie is the artist in the family," Doug whispered.

The kitchen was spotless and smelled like pine-scented room deodorizer. It was hard to believe that dinner would appear anytime soon. But the table in the dinette was set for four and at each place was a cottage-cheese-filled canned peach on a leaf of iceberg lettuce.

Doug's stepfather came in, asked, "Dinner ready?" and sat down. He shook my hand, said, "Hello," and was not heard from during the rest of the meal.

"Lordy," said his mother, "I've been busy as a cat on a hot tin roof today!" She looked at me and confided, "Doug tells me you're quite the cook. I can't compete, but I've made his favorite dish."

That turned out to be her famous chow mein, featuring canned bean sprouts, canned mushrooms, bouillon cubes, and molasses. With dinner we drank hot coffee.

"I like the way you wear your hair," said his mother. "It's so unusual." She gave Doug's stepfather a quick glance and added, "Did Doug tell you that we have a cousin who is Jewish?"

"No," I replied. "He hasn't mentioned that." She looked away and then asked, "Do you understand Doug's art?" I nodded. . . .

"I do admire it!" she said, dishing out seconds. "Looks like we're going to have rain next week." We managed to discuss the weather until it was time for Doug's favorite dessert, apricot-upside-down cake. It was very familiar; my kitchen shelves were lined with canned apricots.

We were out the door by seven. "That went well," Doug said as we left. "My mother likes you."

"How could you tell?" I asked.

"Right now she is saying to my stepfather, 'She seemed like a nice girl.' And he is saying, 'Look who's going to be on *Johnny Carson* tonight! Art Carney!'"

"What would she have done if she didn't like me?" I persisted.

"Nothing different," he admitted. "But I'd know."

Ruth Reichl
Tender at the Bone (1998)

I have a secret

I t is noon on Wednesday and I have a secret.

To the casual observer, everything appears as usual. I peck away on my computer keyboard, interrupted occasionally by the jangle of the phone or the enticing conversation coming from the pod to my right. They laugh, but I am the clever one.

It is noon on Wednesday and I am making dinner.

While the world wobbles, a three-pound London broil cooks slow and low in my new Crock-Pot. I feel a little superior, a little more together knowing that a hearty dinner awaits my family. I will no longer be one of the thousands of Americans who at 5 P.M. still don't know what's for dinner.

I so want my Rival Smart-Pot Programmable Crock-Pot to change my life. I don't want to fret postwork about making dinner or, worse yet, feel guilty because I planned nothing. The science lab corners of the fridge are no place to find nourishment. I envision thoughtful conversations around the table, facilitated by stress-free cooking, to be the coda for our busy day.

I have been watching too much TV.

Janet E. Keeler
"The Crock-Pot That Saved Dinner Time"
Best Food Writing 2001 (2001)

"meat loaf 'n"

After my divorce I got a job and returned to college. I would run home from work to cook dinner for the girls and then hurry back to my night class. After a while, the children grew used to a meal which they called "meat loaf 'n." They got meat loaf 'n potatoes, meat loaf 'n rice, meat loaf 'n raisins (my version of a Middle Eastern dish), and when I was really pressed for time, meat loaf 'n on toast. My children yearned for the gourmet delights of TV dinners. I knew to give the children TV dinners was to neglect them. A mother is supposed to cook. Cooking is the natural sequence to breast-feeding. So it was rarely, and guiltily, that I allowed the baby-sitter to feed them those neat packages. I hoped that in delegating the betrayal they would remember me for the home cooking and the baby-sitter for the ersatz stuff.

Caroline Urvater
"Thoughts for Food"
Through the Kitchen Window (1997)

46

*If it weren't for Philo T. Farnsworth,
the inventor of the television, we'd still
be eating frozen radio dinners.*

Johnny Carson

Intellectual gatherings

Family meals were, for us, intellectual gatherings. I remember watching a television special on President John F. Kennedy, which attributed his success to a family ritual of discussing ideas around the dining table and saying to myself that no one would believe a black family living in a segregated housing project in the South observed the same ritual. What was missing in the television explanation of the Kennedy ritual and present in ours was the magic food and majesty of Mama in her own kitchen. It was a ritual that began during slavery when my ancestors gathered to testify, to bond, to gain strength from one another, to imagine themselves free and empowered. It traveled through time to the housing project of my youth and to Mama's kitchen. It continued when Mama was older and in failing health, with my aunt, her spiritual twin and the family's anchor, preparing the meals that brought us together, but Mama, no less passionate about ideas and polemics, continued to direct us to intellectual dialogue.

Gloria Wade-Gayles
"'Laying On Hands' Through Cooking: Black Women's Majesty and Mystery in Their Own Kitchens"
Through the Kitchen Window (1997)

Mom's cooking was the best

hen we were children Mom fashioned meat loaf or hamburgers, heated canned vegetables or cooked fresh ones till they paled. She was known for her spaghetti: boiled and then overbaked to a gummy mass of indistinguishable pasta, Campbell's tomato soup, and Velveeta processed cheese. We loved it though. My sister, brother, and I thought our Mom's cooking was the best.

Margaret Randall
"What My Tongue Knows"
Through the Kitchen Window (1997)

52

Love from a bowl

On hot nights the lady next door sat her three-year-old twins on the hood of her car and fed them pasta below us. She twirled the spaghetti onto a fork and the girls sucked in their supper strand by strand. The noodles whipped their cheeks with red sauce and made their mother laugh—love from a bowl, in the street, where there was a breeze and people watching.

Theresa M. Maggio
"Love on a Plate"
The Adventure of Food (1999)

How could they possibly
have energy for sex?

I n London I had purchased a few ingredients for an impromptu Indian meal on Crete. My friend's mother, a refined member of upper-class Alexandrian society, was thrilled that I wanted to cook for them. She set the date, cleared the kitchen, pulled out all the pots and pans. She hovered around, asking a steady stream of questions impossible for me to focus on, about Indian geography, Indian customs, Indian cuisine. My friend dutifully translated. Unaccustomed to cooking for others, the food took me all day to prepare. When the meal was finally ready, everyone was ravenous. I served lentils with garlic and yogurt, spicy potatoes, coconut-ginger green beans, cucumber raita, rice, and papadum.

It was a terrible faux pas. Like other Europeans, Greeks make meat the centerpiece of their meal, and my concoctions were entirely vegetarian. Mom could not stop exclaiming at this pitiful version of nourishment. No wonder Indians were emaciated, she thundered. How could they possibly have energy for sex? And still there were eight hundred million of them!

Ginu Kamani
"The Taste of Eros"
The Adventure of Food (1999)

Sugar

Do you know that I once had a theory that if you fed children nothing but nutritious foods, with no additives, preservatives, or sugar, they would learn to prefer those foods? I should have recognized the reality at the first birthday party, when tradition triumphed over nutrition and I made a chocolate cake for the guest of honor. He put one fistful in his mouth and gave me a look I would not see again until I brought a baby home from the hospital and told him the baby was going to stay. The cake look, roughly translated, said, "You've been holding out on me." He set about catching up. The barber gave him lollipops, the dry cleaner a Tootsie Roll. At the circus he had cotton candy, which is the part of the balance of nature designed to offset wheat germ.

The other night for dinner he was having vegetable lasagna and garlic bread, picking out the zucchini, the spinach, even the parsley—"all the green stuff"—and eating only the parts of the bread that had butter. "Know what my favorite food is, Mom?" he said. "Sugar."

Anna Quindlen
Living Out Loud (1988)

The Homesick Restaurant

Now he grew feverish with new ideas and woke in the night longing to share them with someone. Why not a restaurant full of refrigerators, where people came and chose the food they wanted? They could fix it themselves on a long, long stove lining one wall of the dining room. Or maybe he could install a giant fireplace, with a whole steer turning slowly on a spit. You'd slice what you liked onto your plate and sit around in armchairs eating and talking with the guests at large. Then, again, maybe he would start serving only street food. Of course! He'd cook what people felt homesick for—tacos like those from vendor's carts in California, which the Mexican was always pining after; and that wonderful vinegary North Carolina barbecue that Todd Duckett had to have brought by his mother several times a year in cardboard cups. He would call it the Homesick Restaurant.

Anne Tyler
Dinner at the Homesick Restaurant (1982)

Good is good enough

Although Italians are among the most sociable people on earth, genuinely hospitable, and powerfully attracted by the company of others, up to recent times it was quite unusual to be invited to anyone's home for dinner. It was possible, in fact even likely, to be friends for a lifetime yet never eat together, except when eating out.

The family table, worshipfully called *il sacro desco,* was an inviolable place, the one still spot in a turning world to which parents, children, and kin could safely cling. The food put on such a table did not strain for effect, was not meant to dazzle and impress, did not need to be elaborate. It only had to be good. This is still the essential character of *la buona cucina,* of good Italian cooking. Good is good enough.

Marcella Hazan
More Classic Italian Cooking (1978)

The taste of my grandmother's life

When my daddy's mother, Josephine Wilder Hoskins, died in 1985, I inherited her recipes, I who am what became of the little girl who sat at her table. . . . For me, this once-white, plastic-coated-cardboard, double-ring-bound book is magic. Leafing through it leads me back to my grandmother's four-room apartment, to her walnut dining table and her shiny black kitchen table, to the taste of my grandmother's life.

George Ella Lyon
"Just Add Words"
Savory Memories (1998)

Noodle Pudding

Bake @ 350° for 45-50 mts

1 lb wide Noodles
4 Eggs
1/2 cup Sugar
1 DT Sour Cream
1/2 lb Pot Cheese (large curd)
1/2 PT Milk
4 oz Butter
1/2 Jar Orange Marmalade
Vanilla - apples + Peaches

65

I am a turtle

To separate from my culture (as from my family) I had to feel competent enough on the outside and secure enough inside to live life on my own. Yet in leaving home I did not lose touch with my origins because *lo mexicano* is in my system. I am a turtle, wherever I go I carry "home" on my back.

Gloria Anzaldúa
Borderlands/La Frontera (1987)

My mother's voice would dance

I never used to record my mother's cooking lessons, preferring instead to phone her if my memory faltered. Never mind the time difference and the expense of a New Jersey–to–Japan call; my mother's voice would dance as she recounted a favorite recipe, and once again I'd be a teenage girl perched on the counter next to the stove, listening with only half an ear as she imparted the *kotsu* of a dish.

The *kotsu* is the secret step, the key ingredient that makes a recipe special, that takes it beyond the ordinary. "Ginger take smell away." Learning the *kotsu* was the point of every lesson. No cook parts easily with her trove of secrets; that's why they are passed down from mother to daughter, to be kept like jewels within the family.

Lisa Takeuchi Cullen
"The Cooking Lesson"
Best Food Writing 2001 (2001)

It ain't the heat, it's the stupidity

In a house where I often opened a can of tamales for breakfast and ate them cold (I remember sucking the cuminy tomato sauce off the paper each one was wrapped in), Grandma cut out a *Reader's Digest* story on the four major food groups and taped it to the refrigerator. Suddenly our family dinners involved dishes you saw on TV, like meat loaf—stuff you had to light the oven to make, which Mother normally didn't even bother doing for Thanksgiving.

Our family's habit of eating meals in the middle of my parents' bed also broke overnight. Mother had made the bed extra big by stitching two mattresses together and using coat hangers to hook up their frames. She'd said that she needed some spread-out space because of the humidity, a word Lecia and I misheard for a long time as stupidity. (Hence our tendency to say, *It ain't the heat, it's the stupidity.*) It was the biggest bed I ever saw, and filled their whole bedroom wall-to-wall. She had to stitch up special sheets for it, and even the chest of drawers had to be put out in the hall. The only pieces of furniture that still fit next to the bed were a standing brass ashtray shaped like a Viking ship on Daddy's side and a tall reading lamp next to the wobbly tower of hardback books on Mother's.

Anyway, the four of us tended to eat our family meals sitting cross-legged on the edges of that bed. We faced opposite walls, our backs together, looking like some four-headed totem, our plates balanced on the spot of quilt between our legs. Mother called it picnic-style, but since I've been grown, I recall it as just plain odd. I've often longed to take out an ad in a major metropolitan paper and ask whether anybody else's family ate back-to-back in the parents' bed, and what such a habit might signify.

Mary Karr
The Liar's Club (1995)

Things not to be forgotten at a picnic

A stick of horseradish, a bottle of mint-sauce well corked, a bottle of salad dressing, a bottle of vinegar, made of mustard, pepper, salt, good oil, and pounded sugar. If it can be managed, take a little ice. It is scarcely necessary to say that plates, tumblers, wine-glasses, knives, forks, and spoons, must not be forgotten; as also teacups and saucers, 3 or 4 teapots, some lump sugar, and milk, if this last-named article cannot be obtained in the neighborhood. Take 3 corkscrews.

Beverages—3 dozen quart bottles of ale, packed in hampers; ginger-beer, soda water, and lemonade, of each 2 dozen bottles; 6 bottles of sherry, 6 bottles of claret, champagne, and any other light wine that may be preferred, and 2 bottles of brandy. Water can usually be obtained; so it is useless to take it.

Isabella Beeton
Mrs. Beeton's Book of Household Management (1859–1861)

72

Gut-filling meals
of humble means

Patio food of the fifties was like Prozac for the tongue and tummy. Uplifting in almost every respect, lawnside meals of this era kindle warm memories of full stomachs, two-parent families, and apparent emotional harmony. Who can forget these immensely satisfying, gut-filling meals of humble means? Hunks of water-melon, Kool-Aid, sweet corn, green Jell-O molds, and Oscar Mayer wieners would fall off soggy plates and tumble onto the grass, where they became either instant pet food or the buffet for an insect hooten-anny, depending upon the sucrose content of the slippage. Sometimes no larger than ten feet square, the flagstone patio became the modern equivalent of the Neanderthal fire pit: a meeting ground where the raw, the savage, and the cooked came together in the service of family, chow, and masculine gastronomy. It was camp food with all the conveniences.

Gideon Bosker
Introduction
Patio Daddy-O (1996)

My favorite animal is steak.

Fran Lebowitz

The weekend madness, when I went to stay with the rest of the family in their country house, was equally entertaining. Dinner conversation invariably involved discussing the personality of the animals we were eating.

Nicole Alper
"Baguette"
The Adventure of Food (1999)

Convenience foods

A child of the '50s and '60s, I was raised on Minute rice, Campbell's soups, Velveeta cheese, and frozen vegetables—the miracle convenience foods of that era. We ate red meat about five nights a week; on the other two we ate chicken or fish. "Salad" meant iceberg lettuce, hothouse tomatoes, and mayonnaise. Cucumbers were sometimes added, but that was already edging toward the exotic.

Mollie Katzen
The New Moosewood Cookbook (2000)

The family table

As a child growing up in rural Florida, I learned the importance of the family table. It was there that I felt love matched only by my family's appreciation for fresh, wholesome food, a love of good cooking, and a fellowship just not possible at a restaurant table or at the drive-in window of a fast-food outlet. These early experiences started me on my life's journey of cooking for families.

I have cooked for families in times of celebration and times of great sadness, and always these families came together to embrace the food and each other. The table is a place of communion for life's large and small events.

Art Smith
Back to the Table:
The Reunion of Food and Family
(2001)

Refinement and taste

If the truth be known, all affectations and pretense aside, the dinner, the world over, is the symbol of a people's civilization. A coarse and meanly cooked and raggedly served dinner expresses the thought and perhaps the spiritual perception of a nation or a family. A well-cooked and prettily served dinner will indicate the refinement and taste of a nation or a family.

Robert Laird Collier
English Home Life (1886)

Nurturing others

My childhood Sundays served not as a beginning or end of every week, but as the nucleus from which all other days sprang. The parables Grandmother couched as memories, seasoned by the casual ceremonies of ritual meals, incarnated for me the vital significance of tolerance and strength, as well as the importance of integrity gained through nurturing others, family members and strangers alike.

L. Elisabeth Beattie
"Sunday's Legacies"
Through the Kitchen Window
(1997)

Free run of the kitchen

My biggest excitement came each Friday, when my mother would bake a challah (braided egg bread). I was enthralled, and would come in from wherever I was playing just in time to help her braid it. When she or my grandmother would bake desserts from scratch, I would be breathing down their necks with eagerness and fascination. My mother was tolerant and encouraging enough to allow me free run of the kitchen, and I learned early to prepare all the instant foods, but also to experiment and improvise. My focal point, at age nine or ten, was chocolate desserts, and I invented several in earnest. I thank my mother for telling me she liked them.

Mollie Katzen
The New Moosewood Cookbook (2000)

To life

My mother kept her sterling silver in a velvet-lined box. She would take it out and tediously polish it just for the holidays. My mother would polish slowly, thinking maybe this would be the holiday that would work out all right—without "scenes," without tears. Working late into the night in her quiet kitchen, she would infuse hope into the filigreed pattern of the silver with the soft, worn cloth, polishing the veins in the silver leaves, the hard edges of the silver petals on the spout of her teapot. She brought her flowered bone china out of

the glass breakfront, where it usually sat like objets d'art in a museum. Grandma Rae would call.

What should I bring?
Bring yourself.
I'm bringing stuffed cabbage.
Then Grandma Selma would call.
What should I bring?
Bring yourself.
What's Rae bringing?
The next day Grandma Rae and Grandma Selma would put their stuffed cabbages into my mother's oven and

hover over them, each making sure her dish was heated up just right. They would race each other to the table as all sat to eat. The heavy silver clattered on the good china with a satisfying thunk.

Someone would say how good the stuffed cabbage was.

Which one are you eating? Hers or mine?

Back and forth to the kitchen we went for more brisket or tzimmes or the rest of the gravy. Sometimes we finished Grandma Selma's stuffed cabbage before Grandma Rae's.

I brought stuffed cabbage because Rae did.

If everybody jumped off a roof, would you go too?

Then we'd hear over all the noise the clink-clink-clinking of my father's spoon on his crystal glass, just long enough to stop the clamor. He and my grandfathers would make a toast. We'd all raise our glasses. *L'chaim.*

To life.

Nancy Ring
Walking on Walnuts (1996)

I give myself dinner

"Y ou told me how you started to cook," Susan said. "You have never said why you like it."

"I like to make things," I said. "I've spent a lot of my time alone, and I have learned to treat myself as if I were a family. I give myself dinner at night. I give myself breakfast in the morning. I like the process of deciding what to eat and putting it together and seeing how it works, and I like to experiment, and I like to eat. There's nothing lonelier than some guy alone in the kitchen eating Chinese food out of a carton."

Robert B. Parker
Pastime (1991)

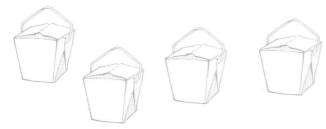

Artificial Cool Whip

We have a friend in Banner Elk who told us this past summer that her youngest daughter, right after her freshman year in college, went to work at a very exclusive inn. She was supposed to be the salad and dessert person. She came home after two or three days there, all excited, and said, "Guess what, Mom, I learned how to make artificial Cool Whip." Her mother said, "You did? How did you make it?" She said, "Well, you buy something at the store called 'whipping cream' and you just whip it and beat it and beat it and beat it and after a while you've got artificial Cool Whip!"

Jane Ellen Stephenson
Table Talk (1995)

That undeniable rock

There we were, solidly one for those moments at least, leaning our arms easily along the cool wood, reaching without thought for our little cups of hot bitter coffee or our glasses, not laughing perhaps as the families do in the pictures and the stories, but with our eyes loving and deep to one another. It was good, worth the planning. It made the other necessary mass meals more endurable, more a part of being that undeniable rock, the Family.

M. F. K. Fisher
The Art of Eating (1954)

Canned goods

At our midwestern dinner table my father's customary question after sampling the green beans was not "When were these picked?" but "What brand are these?" Since he was a grocer who regularly brought home canned goods that had lost their labels, my mother sometimes couldn't answer the question.

Calvin Trillin
Foreword
Recipes from Home (2001)

A wondrous sense of well-being

My grandmother made bread on Saturday afternoons. In her small, bright kitchen, I would watch her mix the dough, forming it into a pale pillow that would rest for some time in the large blue bowl. After an hour, she would uncover the dough and then form it into loaves, each the size of a newborn puppy. Placing them in rectangular bread tins, she would cover each one with a damp dish cloth. On the radiator, they would sleep for two more hours, slowly growing until they doubled in size, rising round and smooth above the rim of the pans.

Once the bread began baking, the house would fill with a wondrous sense of well-being. It was a velvety golden smell that made its way along the corridor and into the farthest room. An aroma that brought such contentment to our home. It was here in Grandma's kitchen that I first learned the pleasure of anticipation. And the paradoxical truth that sometimes the "waiting for" is the very best part.

As Grandma grew older, her loaves became smaller and more dense with crusts as thick as the bark of an oak. But once the bread was baking the aroma and the feeling were always the same. Each loaf of bread was a gift of love that my grandmother gave to our family.

Mary Tiegreen

My father's supper

My father came home from work on weeknights long after we had eaten our supper and gotten into our pajamas. The six of us watched from the living room while he sat at the kitchen table to have his supper. My mother set down his dinner before him, steam rising from the plate she'd kept warm over a pot of boiling water. Loading his fork with his knife, he bent to his dinner, not looking up from the plate until he had pushed it away from him, empty.

Then we could approach him.

Catherine Brady
"Daley's Girls"
I Know Some Things:
Stories About Childhood by
Contemporary Writers (1992)

100

Patty Jean's chitlins

Get a cluster of sisters huddled over stainless sinks and pop in an eight-track of Al Green singing "Love and Happiness," and people you see only at Christmas, Easter, and Juneteenth come out of the woodwork to get a whiff of Patty Jean's chitlins. Whenever we had chitlins at our house, folks my mother wasn't even on speaking terms with just happened to drop by to see how everybody was doing.

Denise Brennen Watson
"False Charms and Chitlins"
Food and Other Enemies (2000)

Casserole dish

I can still see my grandmother, Victoria Giacalone Aprile, climbing our front steps to join us for dinner. It might be Mother's Day, or Christmas Day, or Thanksgiving. The dress might change, the purse, the haircut; but always she carried the same foil-wrapped, dish-towel-insulated steamy casserole dish.

Dianne Aprile
"The Shape of Comfort"
Savory Memories (1998)

A family is what you make it

In truth a family is what you make it. It is made strong, not by number of heads counted at the dinner table, but by the rituals you help family members create, by the memories you share, by the commitment of time, caring, and love you show to one another, and by the hopes for the future you have as individuals and as a unit.

Marge Kennedy and Janet Spencer King
Introduction
The Single Parent Family (1994)

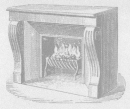

How jolly it was

When supper was finally finished at last, and each animal felt that his skin was now as tight as was decently safe, and that by this time he didn't much care a hang for anybody or anything, they gathered round the glowing embers of the great wood fire, and thought how jolly it was to be sitting up so late, and so independent, and so full.

Kenneth Grahame
The Wind in the Willows (1908)

Acknowledgments

First and foremost, we would like to thank the most magnificent Annetta Hanna, who supported this idea from the get-go. Every author should be blessed with such an editorial angel. Our appreciation to Philip Patrick, who steered us towards publication; and MarySarah Quinn, Maggie Hinders, Liz Royles, and Ronnie Grinberg, who diligently marshaled the book through production.

Thanks also to Laurie Lion at Corbis, who was so very, very helpful to this project. We appreciate the help of all the photographers who submitted photos for our consideration, and thanks go especially to Margaretta Mitchell, Lisa Kereszi, Charles Harbutt, and Joan Lifton, whose wonderful photographs contribute so much to this book.

Thanks go to Janet O'Meara for her wonderful meat loaf; to Jacqueline Pedroli for her exquisite cognac cream sauce; and to Norma Deutsch Sunshine for her life-altering noodle pudding.

We thank our family, friends, and colleagues, and, mostly, we thank our moms for making us the people we are today.

Linda Sunshine and Mary Tiegreen

Summer 2002

Photo Credits

Corbis images: © Bettmann/CORBIS: pp. 24, 37, 49, 63, 96; © CORBIS: pp. 50, 95; © Hulton-Deutsch Collection/CORBIS: pp. 20, 83, 108; © Owen Franken/CORBIS: pp. 66, 91; © Julie Habel/CORBIS: p. 99; © Hurewitz Creative/CORBIS: p. 28; © Minnesota Historical Society/CORBIS: p. 56; © Darren Modricker/CORBIS: p. 102; © Flip Schulke/CORBIS: p. 106; © David Turnley/CORBIS: pp. 6, 104; © Julia Waterlow; Eye Ubiquitous/CORBIS: p. 68; © Jennie Woodcock; Reflections Photolibrary/CORBIS: p. 16.

Charles Harbutt/Actuality: pp. 60–61. Lisa Kereszi: p. 47.

Joan Lifton/Actuality: p. 75. Margaretta Mitchell: pp. 13, 34–35, 84.

Mary Tiegreen: pp. 1, 2–3, 8, 10–11, 14–15, 18, 19, 22, 23, 25, 26, 27, 30, 31, 32, 38–39, 41, 44, 46, 48, 52, 53, 54, 59, 62, 64, 73, 74, 76, 78, 79, 80, 87, 88, 92, 100, 101, 112.

The photos on page 5 are family photos, provided by the authors.

Text Credits

pp. 42–43: From *Tender at the Bone* by Ruth Reichl, copyright © 1998 by Ruth Reichl. Used by permission of Random House, Inc.

pp. 70–71: From *The Liar's Club* by Mary Karr, copyright © 1995 by Mary Karr. Used by permission of Viking Penguin, a division of Penguin Putnam Inc.

pp. 88–89: From *Walking on Walnuts* by Nancy Ring, copyright © 1996 by Nancy Ring. Used by permission of Bantam Books, a division of Random House, Inc.

*People can say what they like about the
eternal verities, love and truth and so on,
but nothing's as eternal as the dishes.*

Margaret Mahy
The Catalogue of the Universe
(1985)